THEN & NOW

MODESTO

OPPOSITE: This photograph of the McHenry Mansion was taken by William Brown in either late 1886 or early 1887. The house on the far left was built by Mrs. J.N. Moad in 1886 and valued at $900 at that time. The McHenry Mansion Foundation purchased this house in 2012 for use as the McHenry Mansion's Visitor's Center and Gift Store.

THEN & NOW

MODESTO

Wayne A. Mathes and
the McHenry Museum

This book is dedicated to Colleen Stanley Bare, Modesto's historian extraordinaire, for her friendship and support in the restoration of the McHenry Mansion and the preservation of Modesto's history.

ISBN 978-0-7385-7485-1

Library of Congress Control Number: 2010942495

Published by Arcadia Publishing
Charleston, South Carolina

Printed in the United States of America

For all general information, please contact Arcadia Publishing:
Telephone 843-853-2070
Fax 843-853-0044
E-mail sales@arcadiapublishing.com
For customer service and orders:
Toll-Free 1-888-313-2665

Visit us on the Internet at www.arcadiapublishing.com

On the Cover: The McHenry Mansion was built in 1883 by Robert McHenry, local rancher and banker. From left to right, this 1893 photograph shows his widow, Matilda; his daughter-in-law Louise; his grandchildren; an unidentified woman; and Augustus Sundstrum, the gardener. In 1976, Aileen and Julio Gallo purchased the mansion and donated it to the City of Modesto to be restored. It is open for tours.

On the Back Cover: Four pillars donated by the Women's Improvement Club (WIC) mark the entrance to Enslen Park, located at Park and Stoddard Avenues.

Contents

Acknowledgments

I would like to acknowledge Janet Lancaster, the McHenry Museum volunteer in charge of the museum's photographic collection, for her suggestions of appropriate photographs for this project and for reviewing the captions. Also, Laura Mesa, McHenry Museum exhibits coordinator (but she does so much more), for scanning all of the "then" images.

It is also important to recognize the work of past historians who have preserved the history of Modesto, beginning with Leonidas Clay Branch in his 1881 publication, *History of Stanislaus County, California;* George H. Tinkman with his 1921 volume, also called *History of Stanislaus County, California;* Sol P. Elias for his 1924 stories, *Stories of Stanislaus;* and Colleen Stanley Bare with her books *The McHenry Mansion: Modesto's Heritage* (1985) and *Modesto Then and Now* (1999). With Sol P. Elias's initial encouragement, Herbert G. Florcken, a professor at Modesto Junior College from 1928 to 1957, spent from 1930 to 1955 compiling a large photographic collection on Modesto. This collection forms the core of the present collection at the McHenry Museum.

Some of the earliest photographs of Modesto were taken by pioneer photographer, William Brown (1838–1893). Brown established a photograph gallery on Front Street, also known as Ninth Street, in 1871. He eventually expanded his business interests to include a large building on the corner of Ninth and I Streets with several retail tenants. He lost the Elaine Block in the November 1881 fire, but rebuilt the structure in brick at the same location. It was also referred to as the Brown and Sayer Building. Another early photographer was Edwin Z. Barnett, who had his photograph gallery on H Street. Some other early photographers of Modesto were Frank H. Hanson, Hanson and Gebhart, Brown and Edwards, Lane and Kiley (of San Francisco), Crigler, Oscar Mayo, and Thomas Shoob.

Greatly enhancing the McHenry Museum's photograph collection was the gift of photographs from Pete Baird. He and his father, Vernon, had a photography studio that operated from the 1930s through the 1990s.

All "then" photographs are in the collection of the McHenry Museum. All "now" photographs were taken by the author.

Introduction

Modesto's founding in October 1870 was not the gradual growth from a general store at a convenient crossroads or ferry, but the full-blown establishment of a thriving community in a few short weeks. Of course, all of this was due to the Central Pacific Railroad coming down through the Central Valley—also known, at the time, as Paradise Valley. Recognizing the importance of a year-round reliable source of transportation by railroad over the seasonal fluctuations of riverboat travel and freighting, the citizens of the neighboring towns of Tuolumne City and Paradise literally picked up their buildings and hauled them to Modesto. A prime example of this is the Ross House. Frank Ross had his hotel cut in two; the first half arrived in Modesto on October 29, 1870, pulled by 60 horses. The second half joined it after some difficulty due to being stuck in sandy soil. The hotel was put back together in time for a grand opening in February 1871 at the corner of Ninth and I Streets.

Modesto was laid out in a grid by Charles Crocker's Contract and Finance Company, the arm of the Central Pacific Railroad that handled such projects. Numbered streets paralleled the railroad tracks, and lettered streets were perpendicular to the tracks. The actual railroad tracks ran between Eighth and Ninth Streets, with Ninth Street being the street where most businesses located. Because Ninth Street fronted on the railroad tracks, it was also known as Front Street. The population continued to increase so that the townspeople could vote Modesto the fifth county seat of Stanislaus County in September 1871. In 1872 and 1873, a new courthouse was erected in the center of the block bounded by H and I Streets and Eleventh and Twelfth Streets. It cost $60,000, including furnishings. At this time, Modesto was considered a wide-open town. Saloons, gambling dens, and houses of ill repute were the norm. As such, the farmhands that harvested the increasingly large winter wheat fields usually ended up being fleeced during their weekend binges. The townspeople's answer to the lawlessness was the formation of the Vigilantes in 1879 and their return in 1884 under the name San Joaquin Valley Regulators. They gave "undesirables" till sundown to leave town, which they did by train, heading off to Oakdale and points south. Modesto was incorporated as a city of the sixth class later that year. In 1888, W.W. Elliott of San Francisco sketched and lithographed a "Birdseye View of Modesto." It reported that 15 trains passed through Modesto each day, and the city had a population of 4,000 inhabitants. Around the map are 22 illustrations of the most important buildings in Modesto and the surrounding area.

Chapter one, "An Instant Village," covers the years 1870–1889 and features most of these buildings. Of all of these structures, only the home of Robert McHenry, now known as the McHenry Mansion, survives today. Chapter two, "A Thriving Town," shows the maturing of the community in the years 1890–1909. Most of the original buildings had been torn down by that time or lost due to fire to be replaced with more substantial brick structures. Tenth Street is becoming the center of the business district. Chapter three, "A City of Civic Pride" (1910–1929), captures the boosterism and sense of community well being that abounded during that time of growth. Notable structures built during this era include the

Modesto Arch, the McHenry Library, the Modesto Hotel, the Hughson Hotel, and the Covell Hotel, the Strand Theatre, and Modesto Junior College. The street scenes show bustling activity. Chapter four, "The Depression and War Years," focuses on the years 1930–1949. Just as Modestoans spent many hours in the 1930s in the town's cinemas enjoying a temporary respite from the struggles of everyday life, during and after World War II, many wounded veterans spent time in Hammond General Hospital recovering from their war injuries.

Chapter five, "All-America City," emphasizes the fun and innocence of growing up in what native-son George Lucas has described as a "Norman Rockwell" town.

The "now" photographs show the profound change that has occurred in Modesto. Hinted at with the creation of McHenry Village in 1952, businesses moved out of the downtown core to shopping centers, strip malls at major intersections, and stand-alone buildings with huge parking lots as far as the eye could see on McHenry Avenue. In the 1960s, the Unsafe Structures Code mandated the demolition of unreinforced brick structures, which doomed such downtown landmarks as Plato's Clothing Store, the Tynan Hotel, the Grollman Building, and Rogers Hall. Left in their places was parking areas or vacant lots. Some have since been built upon—such as the City Tower, which was erected on the former site of the Tynan Hotel—but many lots still remain vacant after 50 years. The emphasis is not on retail but on government buildings such as Tenth Street Place, offices such as City Tower, restaurants such as Galletto Ristorante, and nightclubs such as the Fat Cat. Parking requirements have resulted in large parking structures, such as at Tenth Street Place, the Eleventh Street Garage, the Twelfth Street Garage, and numerous parking lots. Vintage Faire Mall, built in 1977, is now trying to capture the Main Street feel with its concourse of shops adjoining the original structure.

Thinking has come full circle. Modesto, with a population of approximately 215,000, is now trying to revitalize its downtown by creating reasons for people to come there. Successful ventures include the Brenden Theatres, the Gallo Center for the Arts, and events, such as X Fest. There is talk of residential condominiums, redevelopment corridors, and revitalization master plans. It is unfortunate that the old buildings are not around to be rehabbed, repurposed, and restored. They had a lot of character and could have provided a natural theme for the downtown renaissance.

CHAPTER 1

An Instant Village

The Stanislaus County Courthouse is pictured here in 1955. The first unit of the new courthouse built in 1939 is to the far right peeking out from behind the building. The Goddess of Justice atop the building was saved and is now in the lobby of the current courthouse.

This photograph shows a view of the Stanislaus County Courthouse as it faced H Street. It had been constructed in 1872 at a cost of $60,000, including furnishings, from plans designed by architect Albert Austin Bennett. The annex or Stanislaus County Hall of Records was added in 1901. The courthouse park was handsomely landscaped in a symmetrical pattern of walkways that surrounded the building located in the center of the block. It was torn down in 1958 to make way for the present 1960 courthouse by architect Russell Guerne deLappe.

The Elaine Block occupied the northeast corner of Ninth and I Streets. Nathan E. DeYoe and J.S. Riggs were the proprietors of the DeYoe and Riggs Furniture Store (1878–1905). Other businesses included a drugstore, the post office, and a Wells Fargo Express Office. On the second floor was the photography studio of William Brown. Brown constructed this building as a replacement for the wooden structure that burned on November 11, 1881. It was demolished in 1955. The McDonald's restaurant was built in 1999.

The Ross House, considered the finest hotel in Modesto, was moved by Frank Ross from Paradise City to Modesto in 1870 by cutting it in two and reassembling it on the southeast corner of Ninth and I Streets. Ross sold it to James C. Traner, who in turn sold it to Albert Bilicke in 1885 for $9,000. It had 73 guest rooms as well as a dining room, bar, and barbershop. It burned in 1897 and was replaced with a brick hotel, which was demolished in 1965.

The Wood and Turner Hardware store was located at 916–918 I Street. The partnership between Walter B. Wood and Theodore Turner began in 1875 when Turner bought out J.A. Brown's interest in the business. They remained partners until 1898. Theodore Turner was elected the first president of the City of Modesto's Board of Trustees when it became incorporated in 1884. The current building was the home of World Savings for many years. Due to bank mergers, the building is now vacant.

Stimpson Rogers built Rogers Hall in 1877. The main floor held a number of businesses, such as the Gem Saloon, Wells Fargo Express, and the US Post Office. The second floor was a popular venue for many dances, plays, and other performances. A unique feature was its triangular stage set in one corner of the room. It was lighted by gas jets. Rogers Hall was torn down in 1966. The site is now a parking lot for Bank of the West.

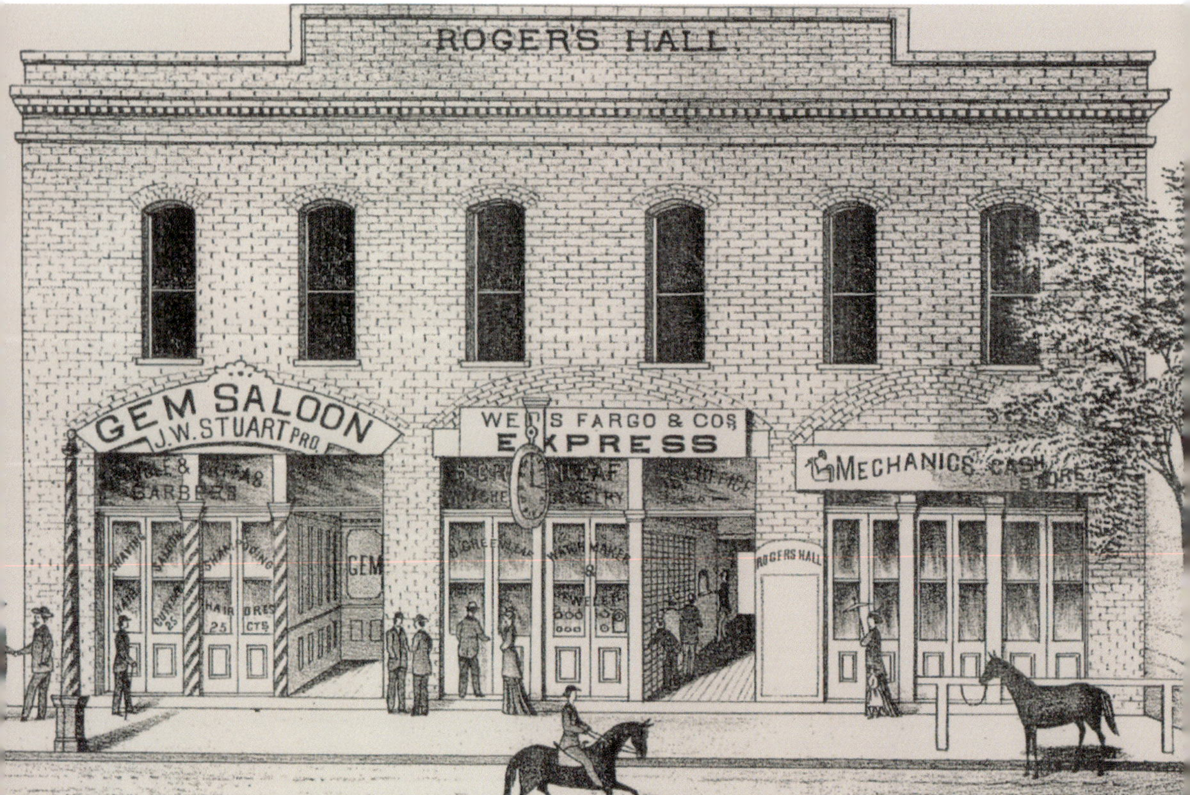

The Modesto Bank, founded in 1878, was located on Ninth Street next to the Ross House. Robert McHenry was one of the six directors and later became the cashier. This building probably burned at the same time as the Ross House in 1897. The Modesto Bank had already moved four years prior to that to a much larger building at the corner of Tenth and I Streets. It was replaced with a single-story brick building, which was demolished in the 1960s.

Edwin Z. Barnett had his photograph gallery on H Street between Tenth and Eleventh Streets. This photograph was taken on July 4, 1890. Barnett participated in the parade as a member of a choral group that subsequently sang at the Fourth's festivities. The *Modesto Evening Herald* began publication in 1875, moving in 1880 to the Braun Building at H and Tenth Streets. Could this have been a free reading room provided by the *Modesto Herald* just up the street from their offices?

Built in 1875 by William Grollman, the Grollman Building housed his harness business with Masonic Lodge rooms on the second floor. It also held the law offices of C.C. Wright, legislator and author of the bill that brought about irrigation to the Central Valley. It was demolished in 1975, and this site became a parking lot until the construction of the Gallo Center for the Arts. This view of the Gallo Center houses the backstage.

This 1885 photograph shows the Modesto Planing Mill at the corner of F and Ninth Streets. The proprietors were A.F. Gilbert and Charles Bennett. According to an advertisement in the Pacific Coast Directory of 1883–1884, they specialized in moldings, brackets, tanks, window frames, wire doors, and screens. They also sold the Althouse Windmill, a vane-less, wooden-bladed windmill. The 1894 Sanborn Insurance map indicates that it was not in operation. It later became part of the Modesto Lumber Company (1878–1994).

The First Presbyterian Church, located at Fourteenth and I Streets, was dedicated on January 2, 1881. Mrs. Robert McHenry and Mrs. J.L. Armstrong led the fundraising drive. Cost of the building, including furnishings, was $4,300. It was replaced by a Mission-style church building in 1911, which contained a swimming pool. It was torn down in 1972. The present building was constructed in 1973 and has had various tenants, such as Safeco Title Company. Rabobank opened a branch in this building in 2009.

The Fourteenth Street School, located on the west side in the middle of the block between H and I Streets, was built in 1874. This two-story brick building consisted of nine rooms and was constructed for $18,000. That first year, there were 278 students. In 1883, a three-year high school program was begun, with 40 students in two of the second-floor classrooms. The building was torn down in 1909. The site is presently that of the *Modesto Bee*.

St. Paul's Episcopal Church was located at the corner of Fourteenth and H Streets. The organization began as a mission in 1879, with actual construction of a building beginning in 1882. It was destroyed by fire on February 9, 1938, and a new church was built where Ralston Towers is located. The property was subsequently leased to the Gilmore Oil Company for $50 per month.

This early-1890s photograph is not a typical view of the McHenry Mansion. It features the trimming of the American elms that were first planted shortly after the mansion was built in 1883. The trellis, leaning away from the mansion, indicates that this pruning effort was not limited to just the trees. Today, the mansion does retain three of the elms on the I Street side. The fence has been replicated, and the I Street porch has been reconstructed.

The Willis Bledsoe house was built at Sixteenth and I Streets in 1885. When Bledsoe came to California in 1862 from Kentucky, he tried mining but gave that up and went into stock raising and wheat farming. He eventually owned 4,480 acres of land. The Judge Frank C. Damrell Building was constructed in 1992–1993. Some of the occupants are the Bank of America and the law firm of Damrell, Nelson, Shrimp, Pallios, Pacher & Silva, which occupies the top floor.

Henry Voight lived at the corner of Sixteenth and J Streets. Originally from Germany, he spent many years at sea. Later, he tried his hand in the goldfields and then captained a boat between Stockton and San Francisco. He subsequently went into farming in the Waterford area. Slater's Furniture moved into the current building in 1953. The previous occupant of this building was the John C. Breuner Furniture Company.

Seated in front of his house at the corner of Ninth and I Streets are William Brown (1838–1893) and his family. Brown came to Modesto in 1871. He established a photography studio on Front Street between I and J Streets, and then moved to the corner of Front and I Streets. His photographs document much of the early growth of the village of Modesto and its inhabitants.

Walter B. Wood, co-owner of the Wood & Turner hardware store, built this house at 814 Twelfth Street in 1877. It was later owned by Harry D. Crow, who owned the Hotel Modesto. When this side of Twelfth Street was slated for development, it was saved from demolition and moved to Nebraska Avenue. The Twelfth Street Parking Garage was constructed on the site in 2006 as part of the half-block makeover.

This photograph features the J.S. Alexander Fourth of July 1890 parade entry. The J.S. Alexander Grain Warehouse can be seen in the background, which was located at the corner of Ninth and I Streets along the railroad tracks. J.S. Alexander was the grand marshal of the parade that year. His float features sacks and sheaves of wheat. Today, Modesto's Transportation Center covers an entire two-block area along Ninth Street, from I Street to K Street.

The Modesto Race Track was established as part of the Stanislaus County Fair in 1875. In 1890, it was much improved and was located along Woodland Avenue, which was then known as Race Track Avenue between the railroad tracks and Barium Avenue (today's Graphics Avenue), almost to Kansas Avenue. In 1904, it was purchased by William and Louise Daggs and became a cattle ranch. The track itself became a vegetable garden.

Modesto's first railroad depot burned in the 1880s, so the freight depot was used for passengers until the new Mission Revival passenger depot was built in 1915. This c. 1907 photograph also shows Modesto's first park at the corner of Ninth and I Streets. The Modesto Arch had yet to be built. The depot burned and was demolished in 1982.

Romulo E. Bangs came to Stanislaus County in 1868 and settled on a 480-acre farm at the corner of Bangs Avenue and McHenry Road. The single-lane dirt road in the foreground is now seven-lane McHenry Avenue and is primarily populated with car dealerships. Bangs grew grain and alfalfa and raised livestock on his farm. He and his wife, Isabella, had seven children.

CHAPTER 2

A THRIVING TOWN

The Modesto Bank building was erected in 1892 at the corner of Tenth and I Streets with the clock tower being added in 1893. It was torn down in 1940 to be replaced by an Art Deco–style bank building in 1941, which is shown on the next page. The Gallo Center for the Arts now occupies this site.

This Art Deco–style bank building was constructed in 1941 by the Anglo California Bank on the site of the Modesto Bank Building. It subsequently became the Crocker Bank and was demolished in 2003. Under the leadership of Marie Damrell Gallo, the Gallo Center for the Arts opened with a splendid gala in September 2007. The center has two theaters: the Mary Stewart Rogers Theater (1,250 seats) and the Foster Family Theater (444 seats).

The Rogers Boy Drinking Fountain was erected in the middle of the intersection of Tenth and I Streets by Caroline Rogers DeYoe in 1893. It was a memorial for her husband, Stephen Rogers; her son, Stimpson Rogers; and her grandson, Stephen Roy Rogers. It bore a statue of her grandson in Carrara marble and had a canopy of California granite. It cost $1,500. In 1906, it was moved to the courthouse park, where it resided until 1953. Pieces of it are in storage. Plans call for its restoration.

John J. McMahon, who was engaged in farming, built his home at 1521 I Street in 1900. He lived there until his death in 1926. McMahon served on the board for the construction of the McHenry Library—a gift of Ora McHenry. His son John Jr. then moved into the house for a few years before residing at the Hotel Modesto. Luther Crabtree opened the Town House Lodge on this corner in 1959. It continues to operate as a Best Western Motel.

The Toggery was a retail men's clothing store located at 815 Tenth Street. The owners were Richard Chester Dozier and Alex Leiter. They opened their business in 1906. The gentlemen pictured in this c. 1910 photograph are probably Dozier, Leiter, and their longtime clerk and tailor, Julius Hansen. Although Leiter died in 1944 and Dozier in 1949, Leiter's son LeVerne carried on the business until it closed in 1960. Today, part of the City Tower is in this location.

The very elegant Tynan Hotel at the corner of Tenth and H Streets opened in 1890 without a third floor or clock tower. This photograph shows it after the clock tower was added to complete the three-story building. The clockworks were never installed, and the tower was removed in 1916. The hotel was torn down in 1961. The City Tower building, constructed in 1993, contains a three-level garage with four floors of offices. The architect was Thom Torvend.

This photograph shows the business of Jones & Stoddard Grocers. It was on H Street as part of the retail space on the ground floor of the Tynan Hotel. Most grocers, at this time, displayed their produce on the sidewalk in front of their establishment. A scale is just visible in the lower-left corner of this photograph and was probably used to weigh commodities, such as potatoes. Robert Elder's tailor shop is next door.

The First Methodist Episcopal Church was built in 1873 at the corner of H and Thirteenth Streets. That edifice was replaced in 1889 only to be rebuilt in 1891 due to a fire. This photograph dates from that time. Other additions were added in 1906 and again in 1911. In 1932, the First Methodist Church moved to its present site at Sixteenth and I Streets.

The Stanislaus County Hospital and Alms House, as it originally was called, was built in 1891 in the Victorian Stick style of architecture. It commanded a grand presence out by the cemeteries on what is now Scenic Drive. A long driveway extended diagonally to the front door. It provided care for the poor and had 19 beds. In 1966, the Stanislaus County Hospital became Scenic General Hospital. The current buildings reflect the diagonal placement of the original structure.

The first Modesto High School sat in the middle of the block bounded by L and M Streets and Twelfth and Thirteenth Streets. It was constructed in 1901 at a cost of $19,500. In 1918, the present Modesto High School was constructed (now greatly enlarged and modified), and this building became Developmental School for junior high students. In October 1926, the name was changed to Roosevelt School. When the current Roosevelt School was built in 1951, this structure was sold as surplus property.

The G.P. Schafer Company was located at the corner of Tenth and I Streets. It opened on May 17, 1900, with six departments carrying dry goods and shoes, clothing, groceries, groceteria, household goods, and a bakery. It was owned by Oramil McHenry but managed by his brother-in-law George Schafer. The business eventually expanded to become one of the largest department stores in the San Joaquin Valley. It closed in 1927. The Bank of Italy (later Bank of America) occupied this site from 1928 to 1981.

On March 17, 1905, Oramil and Myrtie McHenry held a fancy dress St. Patrick's Day party at their home at 906 Fifteenth Street. This photograph was taken in the library. Oramil is dressed as an Indian chief, and Myrtie is seated on the floor as an Indian maiden. The house later became a sanitarium and subsequently apartments. The photograph above shows the now-restored McHenry Mansion library decorated for Christmas, using peacock feathers as the motif.

The Isis Theatre was located at 916–918 Tenth Street. It is listed in the 1911 and 1914 city directories, but not in the 1917 directory. As can be seen, it provided vaudeville acts as well as silent pictures. The Chartreuse Muse, an art gallery featuring local artists and offering art classes, opened in 2008 in this location. The building had long been the home of Rogers Jewelers.

The First Baptist Church erected a concrete building at the corner of Eleventh and K Streets for the sum of $15,000 in 1911. The architectural style the congregation chose reflected a growing trend in church architecture to eliminate the traditional steeple and go with historic revivals—whether it was Mission Revival or crenellated castle motifs. This building was demolished in 1946. The First Baptist Church relocated to its present structure at Needham and Twelfth Streets. The vanished building seen in the image above was replaced with retail stores, reflecting the expansion of Modesto's downtown core.

The Modesto Jail was built of reinforced concrete on H Street between Eleventh and Twelfth Streets probably in 1909. It was decommissioned as the jail in December 1953, but the building was not demolished until July 1974. The current building was constructed in 1976 as the Stanislaus County Administrative Offices until they moved to Tenth Street Place in 1999. It is now occupied by the Stanislaus County Office of Education.

At the intersection where Park Avenue abuts into Stoddard Avenue stand four pillars marking the entrance to Enslen Park. James Enslen gave the Women's Improvement Club $2,000 to purchase 10 acres adjoining Graceada Park for another park. The WIC named the park after him and spent $555 for the pillars made of brick and decorative cement block in 1909. Enslen Park has been formally named a City of Modesto Landmark.

The original Victorian house was the home of Dr. Clayborne Wayne Evans, who began practicing medicine in 1880. The house was located at 1003 Twelfth Street at the corner of J Street. Dr. Jackson C. Robertson, who began practicing medicine in 1906, purchased the home of Dr. Evans in the early 1900s. By 1917, he was using it as his hospital, which he later expanded with an addition on J Street. Robertson's Hospital closed in 1950.

This photograph of I Street looking from Ninth Street towards Tenth Street dates from about 1903. The Rogers Boy drinking fountain is in the center of the intersection of Tenth and I Streets. It was not moved to the courthouse lawn until 1906. The brick building to the right is the Swan Hotel, which replaced the Ross House, which burned in 1897. Schafer's Department Store's sign is prominently displayed on the left side of the street. It opened in 1900.

This c. 1907 photograph shows Tenth Street looking towards I Street from J Street. Due to increased traffic, the Rogers Boy drinking fountain is no longer in the center of I Street. On the left is Schafer's Department Store, and across I Street is the Modesto Bank. On the right is the First National Bank, and across I Street is Lesher's cigar shop and jewelry store. In the distance is the tower of the Tynan Hotel.

This c. 1891 photograph shows Tenth Street looking towards the H Street intersection from G Street. The Tynan Hotel on the left is lacking its third story and clock tower but opened for business in 1890 anyway. The Braun Building to the right was constructed by the brewer, Michael Braun, in about 1878. The *Modesto Herald* newspaper moved their offices to the second floor of this building in 1880. H. and B. Grunbaum had their general store in the IOOF building to the immediate left.

CHAPTER 3

A City of Civic Pride

The Modesto Arch erected over I Street at the Ninth Street intersection was a project of the Modesto Business Men's Association who wanted to promote Modesto. The design and slogan were determined by competitions. Bernard Joseph was selected as the architect, and S.R. Harbaugh came up with the winning slogan. It was constructed in 1912 for $2,000.

The Modesto Arch was moved several feet towards the railroad tracks to accommodate traffic on Ninth Street in 1934. Twenty years later, Stanislaus County celebrated its centennial, as the pictured banner proclaims. A parade and other activities were held as part of the celebration. Efforts to have the arch removed in 1966 were thwarted, and it continues to welcome visitors to Modesto.

The McHenry Library was a gift to the City of Modesto by Oramil McHenry, who died of cancer at age 45. William Henry Weeks was the architect. It was erected at the corner of Fourteenth and I Streets in 1911–1912 with an addition in 1928. The stylish building featured a columned rotunda, three fireplaces, and an auditorium. The McHenry Museum has occupied the building since 1972 and features exhibits on Modesto and Stanislaus County history.

Construction began in 1911 on what was described as the most modern apartment building in Modesto at the corner of I and Fifteenth Streets. G. Lester James owned the 16-unit apartment house until 1942. In the upper left corner of the photograph is the Gustav Bertram house built in 1904. The Parkview Apartments, as they are known today, retain many of its original features, such as the leaded glass china buffets, which swivel to reveal a Murphy bed.

Located in the middle of the block on Tenth Street between H and I Streets was the Cressey Building constructed by C.J. Cressey in 1911. It included retail space on the ground floor and the Alta Apartments up above. The third floor was added at a later time. There were 12 apartments. F.W. Woolworth Company was located at 812 Tenth Street from 1919 to 1948. The Modesto Drug Company was at 824 Tenth Street. The building was torn down in 1975.

The Hotel Modesto was constructed at the corner of Eleventh and H Streets in 1914 by partners Oscar Hogin and Henry T. Crow. Crow later bought out Hogin's interest. A fifth story was added in 1921, with a fireproof addition in 1927. The building burned on May 3, 1944. The lot then became the site of the Modesto City Hall, which opened in 1960. When city hall moved to Tenth Street Place in 2000, the building became offices for the Stanislaus County Court System.

The first Modesto Airport was located at Tuolumne Boulevard and Roselawn Avenue on 74 acres purchased in 1920. The idea of a municipal airport was initially proposed in the city's Charter of 1910—quite forward-thinking for the time. In 1921, it was renamed Coffee Field in memory of Harold "Bud" Coffee, a local pilot who had been killed in a plane crash. In 1933, this land became the nine-hole Municipal Golf Course.

Modesto Junior College was formed in 1921 with South Hall opening in 1923 and North Hall three years later. North Hall was torn down in 1971 and South Hall in 1975 to make way for new construction. Currently, a substantial amount of new construction is under way due to state bond funds. The auditorium has been refurbished and expanded for some $45 million, and a new $19-million student services building was in progress in 2011.

Carl Salber operated a grocery store at the corner of Tenth and J Streets from 1912 to 1914. For many years it was a women's apparel shop. The building lost its dome, and the wood-sash windows were replaced with aluminum sliders. The pointy dome is part of the latest attempt to rehabilitate the building as part of the Tenth Street Place complex. Recently, it has housed a series of restaurants, all of which seem to fail.

The Hotel Hughson at the corner of Tenth and J Streets was constructed by Luella Hughson, widow of Hiram Hughson, and opened on March 6, 1914, with a dinner-dance. Designed by Joseph Bernard, it consisted of six floors and 98 rooms. Its outstanding feature was a blue-tiled swimming pool in the basement. It was demolished in 1998 to make way for the new Tenth Street Place city and county administration offices.

The Strand Theater opened in December 1921 at 1021 Tenth Street with the *Mark of Zorro*, starring Douglas Fairbanks. Constructed at a cost of $250,000, it seated 1,800 people. Besides movies, it had a stage for vaudeville acts and local productions. It burned in 1984. The Brenden Theatres opened on May 14, 1999, with George Lucas's *Star Wars Episode One: The Phantom Menace*. It has 4,000 seats, 18 screens, and was constructed at a cost of $20 million.

Located at Eleventh and J Streets, the Hotel Covell opened on May 1, 1924, with 70 rooms each with a private bath. Owners George and Grace Covell then expanded the building in 1929 with an additional 60 rooms, retail space, and apartments. It was demolished in 1998 to make way for Tenth Street Place. Some of its bricks are engraved and embedded in Tenth Street Place Plaza to raise money for public art projects.

This post office on I Street next to the alley was privately funded by the Modesto Post Office Improvement Association in 1923 and cost $26,000. Ten years later it was replaced with one twice as large as part of the Depression-era Works Projects Administration (WPA) projects to stimulate the economy. It cost $195,000. This was the main post office until 1962 when the Kearny Post Office was built. Now referred to as "El Viejo" or the "old one," the federal government is seeking to sell it.

This c. 1914 photograph features the interurban railway service between Modesto and Stockton. The conductor, with passenger car, is posing on Ninth Street just south of I Street. This railroad service was provided by the Tidewater & Southern Railway beginning in October 1911. The railway was operated by electricity, having some 32 miles of overhead wires. The Tidewater & Southern Railway operated on the Ninth Street tracks until 2000, with the tracks being removed in 2003.

The John Muir School, at 800 East Morris Avenue, opened in 1923. This two-story structure had classrooms lining a central hallway, with a multipurpose room at the far end. After the new John Muir School was constructed, the building became the property of the City of Modesto and was used as offices for nonprofit groups, such as the Girl Scouts and the League of Women Voters. It burned on October 14, 2007, a victim of arson. The property was subsequently sold to the adjoining cemetery.

The Owl Drug Company occupied 936 Tenth Street (at J Street) from 1939 to 1948. F.J. Adair was the manager until 1945, when he opened his own drugstore across the street. P.R. Evey then became the manager. In 1950, Toppers Jewelers moved into the building and stayed there until 1987 or 1988. During that time, the street addresses were changed, and this building became 964 Tenth Street.

This 1925 photograph shows the Richfield Fireproof Garage at the corner of Tenth and G Streets. It was in business from about 1921 to 1933 and provided full service for cars. According to a 1927 advertisement in the Modesto City Directory, this included storage, repairs, battery service, washing and polishing, and greasing. They also sold and serviced Star and Velie automobiles. In later years, the building became a tractor shop, bowling alley, auto supply, boxing arena, and now storage for the Modesto Police Department.

The Covell Garage was located at 1057–1063 Eleventh Street at K Street from 1935 to 1939. Raymond E. Covell was the owner. It provided full car service as well as handled auto sales. As can be seen in the photograph, it pumped Red Crown Gasoline from two pumps under a corner of the building that was left open so that cars could drive through. The building was torn down in 1965. In 1999, the Tenth Street Place parking structure was built.

The J.S. West & Co. was started by James Stuart West in 1909. Originally in the grain and feed business, it expanded into lumber, coal, LP gas, oil, ice, eggs, furniture, and appliances. This filling station was located on H Street between Ninth Street and the railroad tracks. The property is still owned by the J.S. West & Co. The building has been remodeled and is currently being rented to newly-formed religious organizations before they build their own facilities.

The Maze building was located at 817–819 Tenth Street between H and I Streets. The Shackelford-Ullman store moved to this location sometime between 1914 and 1917. It initially was referred to as a dry goods store, but by 1926, the city directories called it a department store. W. Claude Shackelford and Sadie Ullman (later his wife) started the business, which continued until 1941. The shop to the left was a jewelry store.

Chanslor & Lyon Stores, Inc., specializing in auto repair, was located at the corner of Eleventh and J Streets for just a few years beginning in 1933. The building was probably demolished in 1936 because American Trust Company was in the present Art Deco building by 1937. There were several different banks at this location with the last one being Stockton Savings and Loan. It was then converted by Tom Gallo into Galletto Ristorante, which opened in 2001.

The *Modesto Bee* building was located at 815–817 Eleventh Street next to the Hotel Modesto. It was purchased in 1922 for the *Modesto News-Herald*. The presses were located in the basement. McClatchy Newspapers acquired the *Herald* in 1927. After some name changes, it eventually became the *Modesto Bee*. The *Bee* moved to its current location on H Street in 1951. The City of Modesto would eventually acquire the entire block for city hall offices, parking, and additional office space.

CHAPTER 4

THE DEPRESSION AND WAR YEARS

This photograph of the State Theatre was taken on December 7, 1935. Prominently displayed is a large 25¢ sign, the price of admission. This Christmas tree in the lower left corner is awaiting installation. As seen on the marquee, besides the movie, there are cartoons and news.

Opening on Christmas Day 1934, the State Theatre at 1307 J Street featured *Flirtation Walk* with Dick Powell and Ruby Keeler. The State cost $100,000 to construct. The architect was S. Charles Lee, and the local contractor was Harry Brown. In 2005 and 2006, the State Theatre underwent a major renovation. A stage area was added in front of the screen so that it could be used for performances both of local talent and traveling acts. It has a seating capacity of 500 people.

This photograph is of Tenth Street looking from I Street towards J Street and is from the 1930s. The Kress building with its ceramic facade is still there, but many of the single-story businesses next to it now have a uniform top. The Hotel Hughson has been replaced by city and county offices at Tenth Street Place. The facades on the left side of the street also have undergone significant modifications.

This 1930s photograph shows just how extensive this portion of Tenth Street has changed. The foreground is now part of the Modesto Centre Plaza grounds. Where the Strand Theatre is on the right is now Brenden Theatres, and that portion of Tenth Street is now closed to automobile traffic. The Hotel Hughson is now part of the city and county offices at Tenth Street Place.

The Thrifty-Mart Shopping Center opened at the corner of Fourteenth and J Streets in August 1935 at a cost of $85,000. The various departments of the grocery store and other businesses were illuminated with neon lights. Ray W. Jones operated the grocery store. This corner was later taken over by Justensen's Food Stores, managed by J. Alfred Henry.

The Mar-Vell Dress Shop was located in the Hotel Covell retail spaces at the corner of Eleventh and I Streets. It was in business from 1943 to 1964. The proprietress was Gladyce O. Forrest. It specialized in women's fine clothing. Today, Dittos occupies this corner as part of the Tenth Street Place building, which houses city and county offices on its upper floors.

The J.C. Penney Company began construction on a new building in 1947 at the corner of Eleventh and J Streets at a cost of $1 million. Penney's was previously located at 923 Tenth Street. There had previously been a gas station on this corner. Penney's moved to Vintage Faire Mall in 1977. The building was remodeled in 1982 into the City Mall offices for about $100,000.

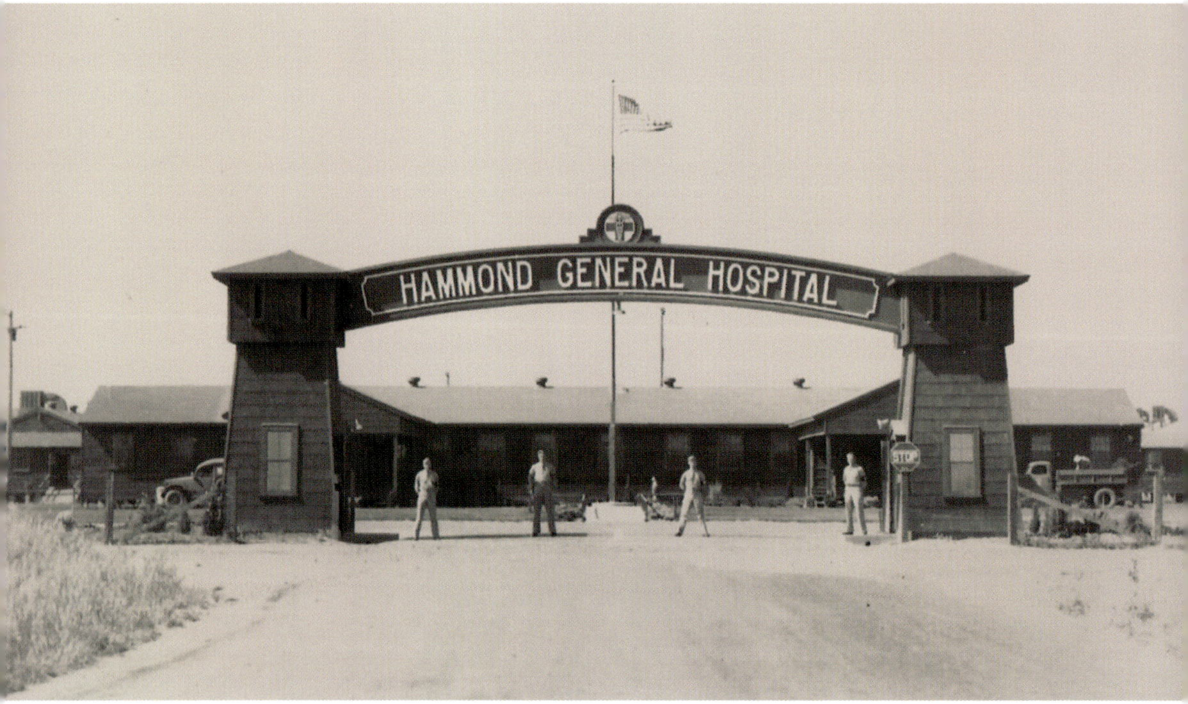

Hammond General Hospital was located on Blue Gum Avenue at Rosemore Avenue and included the area that is now known as the Modesto Junior College West Campus. Opened in 1942, it consisted initially of 113 buildings, which later grew to 177 buildings. Initial construction was $2.6 million. It had 3,000 beds and had served 24,000 injured soldiers by the time it closed in 1945. From 1946 to 1970, as the Modesto State Hospital, it treated some 80,000 mental patients.

The Modesto Court Gas Station, at the corner of O and Needham Streets, was in business for about 10 years, beginning in 1941. At the far right is the tile roof of Pump Station No. 9 at Tenth and Needham Streets. At the far left in the distance is the Modesto Junk Company on Ninth Street. The station seemed to change hands every few years according to the Modesto City Directories. The older cars suggest the austerity of the war years.

Adair's Drug Store, owned by Frederick J. Adair, was at the corner of Tenth and J Streets from about the mid-1940s to the mid-1950s. In the same building but next door was Priester's Town Shop, which featured women's apparel and was at this location from 1926 to 1952. The building was probably constructed in 1926. Sutton's Shoes is to the left of Priester's store. The building has undergone some modification, with most of the exterior architectural detail removed or covered over.

CHAPTER 5

ALL-AMERICA CITY

As the banner from the Modesto Arch proclaims, Modesto was named an All-America City in 1954. The All-America City program was a national competition that recognized the excellence of cities in addressing local issues. Modesto also won this recognition in 1972.

Modesto City Hall was located at 717 Tenth Street. The building had originally been part of the Modesto Fire Department. In this 1954 photograph, Mayor Harry Marks is recognizing Modesto's selection as an All-America City. The vacant Esquire Theatre, originally known as the Lyric Theatre, stands to the right in the photograph. This side of Tenth Street was torn down in the 1960s and has remained a combination of vacant fields and parking lots ever since.

McHenry Village Shopping Center signaled a new trend in shopping for Modesto—the stores were not downtown. The center opened in October 1953 at 1700 McHenry Avenue with 18 stores on some 35 acres. It has since grown to over 70 stores and restaurants. Some of the notable stores were Dunlap's Department Store, which opened in 1958, and Keller's Gifts, which relocated to the center in 1978. Valley Sporting Goods moved into the old Dunlap's space in July 1993.

This January 1953 photograph shows the ground-breaking for Modesto's first strip mall at Orangeburg and College Avenues. Developed by Giddings Brothers, it took five years to complete. Early businesses included Angelo's San Francisco Market (No. 2), Blewett's Ice Cream Shop, Bradbury Cleaners, Turner's Hardware Company, Keller's Variety Store, Paul's Rexall Drugs, Lullaby Land, Priester's Department Store, Roman's Hairdressing, and the Roosevelt Center Barbershop.

Burge's Drive-in was located at 1514 Ninth Street at the corner of O Street from 1948 to 1966. Edward Burge was the owner. This photograph originally appeared in the 1948 *Buccaneer,* the yearbook of Modesto Junior College. Hamburgers were 30¢, cheeseburgers were 40¢, and Cokes were 10¢. The most expensive item on the menu was a New York Cut Steak with salad and shoestring potatoes for $1.90. Burge's Drive-in also served breakfast.

The Felix Drive-in was a typical high school hangout. It opened at the corner of Alice Street and McHenry Avenue in 1958. The owner was Leonard Felix, who had previously operated Al's Drive-in. He subsequently sold it to Arlin and Betty Young. By 1963, it was closed. The site's most recent occupant, a Mexican fast-food restaurant, failed; the building currently lies vacant.

This photograph shows Tenth Street looking from K Street towards J Street. A very popular pastime for teenagers in the 1950s was "dragging Tenth," as cruising was then known in Modesto. Beginning at around 8:00 p.m., as many as 300 cars would follow the same route down Tenth Street to G Street, turn around in a lot, come back up Tenth Street to O Street, turn around again at Burge's Drive-In, and then repeat the whole process.

This photograph shows Tenth Street looking from J Street to K Street during the holidays in about 1959. Tenth Street is now a one-way street with the traffic coming towards the camera. The route for "dragging" in Modesto shifted from just Tenth Street to include Eleventh Street in order to complete the loop. Native-son George Lucas based *American Graffiti* on his experiences dragging in Modesto. Set in 1962 but shot in 1972, most of the movie was filmed in Petaluma because much of Tenth Street had dramatically changed in appearance over the previous decade.

The Mayflower was in business at 310 McHenry (at the corner of Almond Street) from 1940 to 1976. Prior to that, it had been located at 1013 Tenth Street. The neon sign in the window advertises homemade candy. Nicholas G. Yialouris, the proprietor, was known for his hand-dipped chocolates. Many downtown stores gave his chocolates as gifts to their customers at Christmas.

This photograph is looking north on McHenry Avenue from Morris Avenue. In the 1970s and 1980s, McHenry Avenue replaced the downtown for cruising. The one special night that everyone turned out to cruise was on the Saturday after high school graduation. Thousands of people would line McHenry Avenue for Graffiti Night. After a series of incidents, including one shooting, cruising was banned in Modesto in 1990.

This 1970s photograph shows the USA Gasoline station at the corner of McHenry Avenue and Briggsmore Avenue. This corner is now occupied by landscaping of the Briggsmore Square development. In the distance are the water plumes of the Burchell Fountain. The Goodyear building has been replaced by Village West, a shopping center anchored by a Rite-Aid Pharmacy. Gas stations are now self-service, with the cashier in a small booth.